EXPANDED EDITION
Grade
2

The *Science Mysteries* lesson is part of the Picture-Perfect STEM program K–2 written by the program authors and includes lessons from their award-winning series.

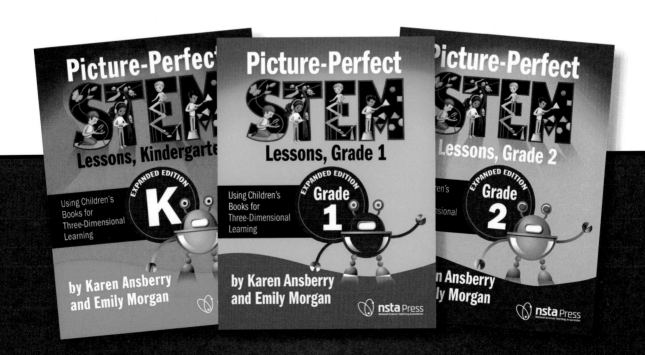

Science Mysteries

Description

After reading a story about an extraordinary young scientist, students are engaged in solving a mystery that involves exploring properties of matter. Students conduct an investigation, use science practices to gather evidence, and use that evidence to support their claim about the identities of two mystery mixtures.

Alignment with the *Next Generation Science Standards*

Performance Expectation		
2-PS1-1: Plan and conduct an investigation to describe and classify different kinds of materials by their observable properties		
Science and Engineering Practices	**Disciplinary Core Idea**	**Crosscutting Concepts**
Asking Questions and Defining Problems Ask and/or identify questions that can be answered by an investigation. **Planning and Carrying Out Investigations** Plan and conduct an investigation collaboratively to produce data to serve as the basis for evidence to answer a question. **Engaging in Argument From Evidence** Construct an argument with evidence to support a claim.	**PS I.A: Structure and Properties of Matter** Different kinds of matter exist and many of them can be either solid or liquid, depending on temperature. Matter can be described and classified by its observable properties.	**Energy and Matter** Objects may break into smalller pieces:, be put together into larger pieces, or change shape. **Patterns** Patterns in the natural and human-designed world can be observed, used to describe phenomena, and used as evidence.

Note: The activities in this lesson will help students move toward the performance expectation listed, which is the goal after multiple activities. However, the activities will not by themselves be sufficient to reach the performance expectation.

Featured Picture Books

TITLE: **Ada Twist, Scientist**
AUTHOR: **Andrea Beaty**
ILLUSTRATOR: **David Roberts**
PUBLISHER: **Abrams Books for Young Readers**
YEAR: **2016**
GENRE: **Story**
SUMMARY: *In this charming story about a girl on a mission to use science to understand her world, young Ada discovers that her boundless curiosity can help her solve one smelly mystery!*

TITLE: **Matter**
AUTHOR: **Abbie Dunne**
PUBLISHER: **Capstone Press**
YEAR: **2016**
GENRE: **Non-Narrative Information**
SUMMARY: *In this colorful, photo-packed book, young readers will learn about the properties of solids, liquids, and gases—how they can be mixed together and how they can change from one form to another.*

Time Needed

This lesson will take several class periods. Suggested scheduling is as follows:

Session 1: Engage with *Ada Twist, Scientist* Read-Aloud and Great Scientists Chart

Session 2: Explore with Properties of Matter and **Explain** with Our Results

Session 3: Explain with Properties of Matter Vocabulary and *Matter* Read-Aloud

Session 4: Elaborate with Mystery Mixtures

Session 5: Evaluate with Matter Quiz and Matter Mystery

Materials

For Great Scientists Chart (per student)

• 1 pack of sticky notes

For Properties of Matter (per student)

• Hand lens
• Safety goggles

For Properties of Matter (per group of 4 students)

• Small tray containing the following materials:
  • 4 plastic 3 oz cups, each half-filled with a different substance: salt, cornstarch, white sand, and baking soda (Use a permanent marker to label each cup with the name of the substance.)

- 1 small, plastic, lidded container filled with approximately ½ cup of water (labeled and closed)
- 1 small, plastic, lidded container filled with approximately ¼ cup of vinegar (labeled and closed)
- 2 plastic 5 ml eyedroppers (1 dedicated to each liquid)
- 4 teaspoons (1 dedicated to each solid)
- 16 wooden, noncolored craft sticks for stirring (4 per student)
- 16 plastic 3 oz bath cups (4 per student)

Note: The following quantities should provide enough for four classes

- 1 lb. of salt
- 1 box of cornstarch (12 oz)
- 1 lb. of white sand (Use a fine, crystalline sand for best results. Ashland decorative stone granules [1.75 lbs] are available in white at Michael's craft stores.)
- 1 box of baking soda (12 oz)

For Properties of Matter Vocabulary (per student)

- Vocabulary cards (1 strip of cards, precut)
- Tape or glue

For Mystery Mixtures (per student)

- Hand lens
- Safety goggles

For Mystery Mixtures (per group of 4 students)

- Small tray containing the following materials:
  - 2 plastic 3 oz bath cups, each half-filled with a different "mystery mixture": equal parts cornstarch and sand (mixture A), and equal parts salt and baking soda (mixture B) (Use a permanent marker to label each cup "Mystery Mixture A" or "Mystery Mixture B.")
  - 1 small, plastic, lidded container filled with approximately ½ cup of water (labeled and closed)
  - 1 small, plastic, lidded container filled with approximately ¼ cup of vinegar (labeled and closed)
  - 2 plastic eyedroppers (1 dedicated to each liquid)
  - 2 teaspoons (1 dedicated to each mystery mixture)
  - 8 wooden, non-colored craft sticks for stirring (2 per student)
  - 8 plastic 3 oz bath cups (2 per student)

For STEM Everywhere (if you wish to send the materials home with each student)

- Food coloring
- 2 cups cornstarch
- Aluminum foil pie pan

Student Pages

- Properties of Matter data sheet
- Properties of Matter testing mat
- Vocabulary Cards
- New Vocabulary List
- Mystery Mixtures data sheet
- Mystery Mixtures testing mat
- Matter Quiz
- Matter Mystery
- STEM Everywhere

Background for Teachers

Matter is all around us. Matter is defined as anything that has mass and takes up space. The paper this book is written on, the water in your bottle, the air you are breathing—they are all made of matter! So what is matter made of? All matter is made of tiny *atoms*. They are so small that you cannot see them with your eyes or even with a standard microscope. Atoms combine to form *molecules*, and these molecules make up a variety of substances. Matter can be described by its properties. Some properties of matter include color, texture, hardness, solubility (ability to dissolve in other substances), reactivity (ability to chemically react with other substances), and state.

Most matter on Earth is found in one of three states: solid, liquid, or gas. In this lesson, students find examples of all three states of matter as they observe common household substances such as salt, sand, baking soda, cornstarch, water, and vinegar. Each state of matter can be identified by its distinctive properties of shape and volume. A *solid* has a definite shape and a definite volume. Its molecules are the most tightly bound together of the three main states of matter. Solids can be poured only if they are made of very small particles such as salt crystals, grains of sand, or powdered substances. Up close, salt crystals look like tiny cubes. Their flat surfaces reflect light, so they look somewhat shiny. Sand, depending on its mineral composition, may be a mixture of different-shaped crystals and more irregular grains. A powder, such as baking soda or cornstarch, is a dry solid composed of a large number of very fine particles that may flow freely when tilted or poured.

A *liquid* has a definite volume, but its shape changes more readily because its molecules are more loosely bound together than those of a solid. A liquid, whether it is thick or thin, is a wet substance that can be poured and always takes the shape of its container. A *gas* has no particular shape or volume. It will expand to fill the space it is in. It can also be compressed to fit a smaller container. Gas has this property because the distances between the molecules of a gas are much greater than the distances between the molecules of a solid or a liquid. A bubble is a thin sphere of liquid enclosing air or another gas such as water vapor or carbon dioxide. Much of the universe is composed of a fourth state of matter known as *plasma*. Plasma has properties different from the other three fundamental states of matter. Scientists can generate plasma in a lab, and it naturally exists inside stars.

Matter can be combined in different ways. A *mixture* is made up of two or more different substances that are mixed but not combined chemically. Mixtures can be solids, liquids, or gases in any combination. Sand and salt stirred together is a mixture. Food coloring in water is a mixture. Air is a mixture of gases. One particular type of mixture is called a *solution*. In a solution, one substance is evenly mixed

with another, making the particles of the substance too small to be seen or filtered out. Salt [dissolved] in water is a solution. The salt disappears, but it is still there. If you tasted the solution, it would taste salty. This mixture could be separated by heating the water until it evaporates, leaving behind the salt crystals.

Matter can also be combined chemically. When two or more substances are mixed, a new substance with different properties may be formed. This process is called a *chemical change*. Chemical changes create entirely new substances. After a chemical change occurs, physical methods, such as drying or filtering, cannot undo the change. In a chemical change, the molecules of different materials rearrange to form entirely new *compounds*. The new compounds have different properties. For example, when vinegar and baking soda are mixed, a chemical change occurs and a new substance—carbon dioxide gas—is formed.

In this lesson, students perform tests on some common household substances to observe their properties. In the process, they learn that matter can be described and classified by its observable properties and that matter can be a solid, liquid, or gas. An equally important component of this lesson is students learning about the practices of scientists. By engaging in science and engineering practices (SEPs) to observe the properties of matter (and eventually solving a mystery), students learn firsthand how scientists ask questions, carry out investigations, and support their claims with evidence. Students are also introduced to the crosscutting concept (CCC) of energy and matter as they use their senses to make observations of different kinds of matter and the CCC of patterns as they recognize how patterns in certain substances appear and behave.

Learning Progressions

Below are the disciplinary core idea (DCI) grade band endpoints for grades K–2 and 3–5. These are provided to show how student understanding of the DCI in this lesson will progress in future grade levels.

DCI	Grades K–2	Grades 3–5
PS1.A: Structure and Properties of Matter	• Different kinds of matter exist and many of them can be either solid or liquid, depending on temperature. Matter can be described and classified by its observable properties.	• Measurements of a variety of properties can be used to identify materials.

Source: Willard, T., ed. 2015. *The NSTA quick-reference guide to the* NGSS: *Elementary school.* Arlington, VA: NSTA Press.

engage

Ada Twist, Scientist Read-Aloud

**Inferring**

Show students the cover of *Ada Twist, Scientist* and introduce the author, Andrea Beaty, and illustrator, David Roberts. *Ask*

? Based on the cover, what do you think this book might be about? (a girl who likes science or is a scientist)

? How do you know? (from the title, the goggles she is wearing, or the pictures in the background)

? What do you think the tennis player on the cover has to do with the story? (Answers will vary.)

**Questioning**

Connecting to the Common Core
Reading: Literature
KEY IDEAS AND DETAILS: 2.1

Read the book aloud, then *ask*

? Who is the tennis player on the cover? (Ada's brother)

? What mystery did Ada try to solve? (the source of the horrible stench)

? How did she try to solve it? (She wrote down lots of questions and then tested different smells with her homemade sniffing machine.)

? By the end of the story, did Ada solve the mystery? (no)

? Do you think scientists always find the answers to their questions? (Answers will vary.)

? The book says, "But this much was clear about Miss Ada Twist: She had all the traits of a great scientist." What are the traits of a great scien-

tist? In other words, what are great scientists like? (Answers will vary.)

? How was Ada a great scientist? (Answers will vary but may include being passionate about understanding the world around her, being curious or asking questions that lead to more questions, making observations, doing research, performing tests and experiments, persevering, etc.)

? Look back at page 18. What safety equipment does Ada wear to help her do science safely? (She wears safety goggles and gloves and also has her hair pulled up.)

? Look back at page 29. What other tools or equipment do you see in the picture that Ada might use to help her do science? (books, models, beakers and flasks, microscope, screwdriver, etc.).

? Ada is holding one of the most important tools of a great scientist. What is it? (pen, pencil, or marker)

Explain that great scientists use pencils (and technologies such as computers) to write down their

ENGAGING WITH ADA TWIST, SCIENTIST

GREAT SCIENTISTS CHART

questions, plan their investigations, record their data and conclusions, draw sketches and diagrams, make claims supported by evidence, and compose research papers to share with other scientists. Good communication in all forms, not just writing, is one of the most important skills great scientists can have. Scientists also need to be team players!

Great Scientists Chart

Make a whole-class chart titled "Great Scientists…," and *ask*

? What great scientists do you know of? (Answers will vary.)

? What are some of the skills or characteristics of great scientists? (Answers will vary.)

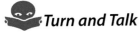 *Turn and Talk*

Next, have students turn and talk with a partner to come up with a few words that describe what great scientists are like or what they do in their work. Pass out sticky notes, and have each pair of students write their words or phrases on separate sticky notes and put them on the chart. Then

put similar words and phrases together and look for common themes such as "Great scientists… make observations," "Great scientists… are curious," "Great scientists… ask questions," or "Great scientists… use safety equipment."

Next, *ask*

? Would you like to be a great scientist? (Answers will vary, but many students will likely say yes!)

explore

Properties of Matter

Tell students that you have a problem: You mixed some household substances for a science activity, but you forgot to label your mixtures. Show them two containers of white mixtures. Explain that Mystery Mixture A contains two substances, and Mystery Mixture B contains two other substances. Tell them you need the help of some great scientists to figure out what's what. Like Ada Twist, they are going to use the skills of a great scientist to solve this mystery! Tell them that the first thing they will need to do is find out more about the four substances that you used in the mixtures by observing each substance's individual properties.

> **SEP: Asking Questions and Defining Problems**
> Ask questions that can be answered by an investigation.

Show students the labeled containers of salt, cornstarch, white sand, and baking soda. Tell them that these were the four household substances that you used in the mixtures. *Ask*

? What does "property of a substance" mean? (its characteristics or attributes)

? What properties of these substances could we safely observe? (what they look like [color, grains, etc.] and how they feel [texture, etc.])

? What are some ways that we can safely observe these substances? (look at them with a hand

OBSERVING MATTER

lens or microscope, touch them but do not taste them, etc.)

Arrange students into teams of four. Pass out a Properties of Matter data sheet student page, a Properties of Matter testing mat student page, a pair of goggles, and a hand lens to each student. Then review the safety guidelines for observing and testing the substances in this activity. Tell students to use their best powers of observation!

Now, have one person from each team go to the materials table and carefully carry a tray of materials back to his or her team. Tell students to wait until every team has its materials, and then you will go over the testing procedure together. Explain that their task is to be like Ada Twist, scientist, and ask questions and make observations while exploring the substances. Like Ada, they will also be following safety guidelines.

The first thing students should do is place a small plastic bath cup on each empty circle of their testing mat, which has circles labeled "salt," "cornstarch," "sand," and "baking soda." They should also place a craft stick next to each cup to use for stirring (stirring the water into the substance first, then stirring the vinegar into the substance and water). The purpose of the mat is to help the students identify the substance they are testing and allow for easy cleanup. After the activity, the plastic cups, substances, craft sticks, and mat can be tossed into the trash.

SEP: Planning and Carrying Out Investigations
Plan and conduct an investigation collaboratively to produce data to serve as the basis for evidence to answer a question.

Tell students that you will all test the first substance together to learn the process. Have students take turns putting one *level* teaspoon of the salt from the plastic cup labeled "salt" into the corresponding cup on their testing mat. Remind them not to use this spoon for any other substance to avoid contamination. Tell students that they will record their observations on their Properties of Matter data sheet. Then begin the testing as follows:

Test 1: Rub the substance between your fingers. How does it feel? Record the texture. (Students may describe the salt as rough, hard, gritty, etc.)

Test 2: Use a hand lens to look more closely at the substance. Can you see any crystals? Write yes or no. (Explain that crystals can look like tiny cubes or other shapes with flat sides. Their flat surfaces reflect light, so they may look somewhat shiny. The sand, depending on its mineral composition, may be a mixture of different-shaped crystals and more rounded grains.)

Test 3: Use an eyedropper to add three full droppers of water (3 teaspoons or 15 ml) to the substance. (Remind students not to use this eyedropper with the vinegar to avoid contamination.) Stir with a craft stick for 30 seconds and observe if the salt appears to disappear, bubble, thicken, or do something else. (Most of the salt should eventually dissolve and disappear, but it is not important for students to use or understand the word *dissolve* at this point. They can also describe how the water appears [e.g., stays clear, turns cloudy, etc.].)

Test 4: Use an eyedropper to add 10 drops of vinegar to the same cup. (Remind students not to use this eyedropper with the water to avoid contamination.) Stir with a craft stick for 30 seconds and observe if more of the salt appears to disappear, bubble, thicken, or do something else. (A little more of the salt might eventually dissolve, but they

should not observe bubbling. Students will most likely observe nothing happening.)

After testing the salt, *ask*

? What else did you notice about the salt? (Answers will vary.)

? What questions do you have about the salt? (Questions will vary.)

Then have students test the other three substances following the same procedure. Remind them of the safety guidelines as they work. A sample completed data table is shown in Table 11.1 (observations may vary).

explain

Our Results

**Turn and Talk**

After students have finished testing all four substances, have them turn and talk with a partner to compare the results of their tests. Then *ask*

? What interesting observations did you make? (Answers will vary.)

Table 11.1. Sample Completed Data Table for Properties of Matter

Test	Salt	Cornstarch	Sand	Baking Soda
1. Texture (feel)	Rough and gritty	Slippery	Rough and gritty	Smooth
2. Crystals? (yes/no)	Yes	No	Yes	No
3. What happens with water?	Salt disappears, and water looks almost clear.	Water turns milky.	Sand does not disappear, and water looks cloudy.	Baking soda disappears, and water looks cloudy.
4. What happens with vinegar?	Nothing	Nothing	Nothing	Bubbles

? Were any of your results different from the other scientists' at your table? If so, why do you think so? (Answers will vary.)

? What do you think happened to the salt when you mixed it with the water? (Answers will vary.)

? What do you think happened to the cornstarch when you mixed it with the water? (Answers will vary.)

? What do you think happened to the sand when you mixed it with the water? (Answers will vary.)

? What did you notice when you added the vinegar to the baking soda? (It bubbled.)

? What else are you wondering about the substances? (Answers will vary.)

Explain that many of these questions will be answered through reading a nonfiction book during the next class period. Tell students to keep their Properties of Matter data sheets in a safe place because they will be referring to them later. Have students clean up by returning the tray of materials and stacking their cups. Then have students fold up their mats with the craft sticks inside and dispose of them in the trash. Students should wash their hands after they clean up.

Properties of Matter Vocabulary

New Vocabulary List

Tell students that they will be learning some new vocabulary that will help them learn more about properties of matter. Give each student a set of five precut Vocabulary Cards (*gas, solid, dissolve, matter,* and *liquid*). Explain that all of these vocabulary words relate to the things the students observed in the Properties of Matter activity. They may be familiar with some of the words, but some may be new. Have students read each word aloud, then give them time to discuss with a partner what they think each word means.

Next, pass out the New Vocabulary List student page to each student. A new vocabulary list is a "guess and check" type of visual representation. Students develop new vocabulary as they discuss or write their ideas about an unfamiliar word's meaning, read or hear the word in context, and then discuss or write their new understanding of the word. Read aloud each definition in the "What It Means" column, and then have students place each card where they think it belongs in the "Word" column. Tell them that at this point, it's OK to make a guess if they don't have much prior experience with the word. They will be able to find out if their prediction about each word's meaning is correct by reading the book *Matter*. During the read-aloud, they will be able to move their cards to the correct spot on the New Vocabulary List.

Matter Read-Aloud

Using Features of Nonfiction

Connecting to the Common Core
Reading: Informational Text
CRAFT AND STRUCTURE: 2.4, 2.5

Tell students you would like for them to signal (by touching one of their ears) when they hear a word on their vocabulary list as you read the book aloud. Introduce the author, Abbie Dunne, as you show students the cover of the book. Then have them identify the table of contents, title page, glossary, index, and back cover as you flip through the book. *Ask*

? Is this book fiction or nonfiction? (nonfiction)

? How do you know? (It has photographs, a table of contents, glossary, index, etc.)

Read the book aloud, stopping at each page containing one of the new vocabulary words. After reading the word in context, read the glossary definition for the word as well. (The definitions on the New Vocabulary List are a combination of the in-text definitions and the glossary definitions.)

Table 11.2. Sample Completed Table for Matter *Read-Aloud*

Word	What It Means	Examples from The Text	Examples from The Activity
1. *Matter*	Anything that has weight and takes up space	Bed, books, me	Everything
2. *Solid*	Matter that holds its size and shape	Rocks, ice cubes, metal	Salt, cornstarch, sand, baking soda
3. *Liquid*	Matter that is wet and takes the shape of its container	Milk, water, shampoo	Water, vinegar
4. *Gas*	Matter that has no shape and spreads out to fill a space	Air	?
5. *Dissolve*	To mix a substance into a liquid until you can no longer see it	Salt dissolves in water.	Salt and baking soda dissolve in water.

Have students move their cards (if necessary) to the correct places on the New Vocabulary List. Then have them write a few examples from the text for each word in the "Examples from the Text" column. Refer students to their Properties of Matter data sheet and write one or more examples for each word in the "Examples from the Activity" column. When you get to *gas*, students will likely not know what kind of gas is inside the bubbles they observed, so leave that space blank until after the *Matter* read-aloud. Repeat these steps for each word. Table 11.2 shows the answers.

**Questioning**

Connecting to the Common Core
Reading: Informational Text
KEY IDEAS AND DETAILS: 2.1

Ask

? How did the book say you could tell if the salt is still in the water after it dissolves? (You could taste the water. The water would taste salty.)

Explain that when something dissolves, it seems to disappear. You can no longer see it, but it is still there. For example, if you stir salt into water and it dissolves completely, you would no longer be able to see the salt. The solution of salt and water would taste salty, although good scientists don't taste their experiments! If you stir sand into water, it would not dissolve. You would still be able to see the sand.

Then *ask*

? What did you notice when you added the vinegar to the baking soda? (It bubbled.)

? What kind of matter do you think was inside the bubbles? (Answers will vary.)

Explain that bubbles are filled with gas. For example, when you blow a bubble with chewing gum, you are filling it with a gas (your breath). When you blow a bubble with a bubble wand, you are filling it with a gas, too. Also, when you see bubbles inside boiling water, those are filled with gas (water vapor, which is an invisible form of water). In the activity, students dripped vinegar onto baking soda and saw bubbles. Explain that when vinegar and baking soda are mixed together, they combine to form a new substance with new properties—a gas called carbon dioxide, or CO_2. This gas forms bubbles. However, if you could pop the bubbles, the invisible carbon dioxide gas inside would have no shape and would spread out into the room. Carbon dioxide is one of the gases that make up the air we breathe. Have students add carbon dioxide (or CO_2) as an example of a gas to the "Examples from the Activity" column of their New Vocabulary List. Finally, have students tape or glue the Vocabulary Cards to the proper spaces on the student page.

SAFETY

- Wear your safety goggles at all times.
- Do not taste or sniff any of the mixtures.
- Do not pour any of the mixtures or liquids out of the containers. Use only the spoon or eyedropper that is assigned to each substance to avoid contamination.
- You will be touching the mixtures with your fingers. Do not put your fingers near your face after touching them. When the activity is over, you must wash your hands with soap and water.
- You will be using a hand lens to observe the mixtures. Do not let the hand lens touch the mixture. Put your eye as close to the lens as possible, and lean over the cup until the mixture comes into focus. Try closing the eye that is not close to the lens to get a better view.

elaborate

Mystery Mixtures

Tell students that now that they have made observations of the properties of each substance, they can use that information to figure out the contents of Mystery Mixture A and Mystery Mixture B! In other words, they can apply what they learned about the properties of the four different household substances to solve the mystery. They will be working with the same team they worked with for the Properties of Matter activity. Explain that they will need to refer to their Properties of Matter data sheet to compare the results of the tests on the known mixtures with those of the tests on these unknown mixtures. Then pass out a Mystery Mixtures data sheet student page, a Mystery Mixtures testing mat student page, a pair of goggles, and a hand lens to each student. Review the safety guidelines for observing and testing the mystery mixtures in this activity. Tell students to use their best powers of observation!

MYSTERY MIXTURES

Table 11.3. Sample Completed Data Table for Mystery Mixtures

Test	Mystery Mixture A	Mystery Mixture B
1. Texture (feel)	Rough, gritty, and slippery	Rough, gritty, and smooth
2. Crystals? (yes/no)	Yes (some)	Yes (some)
3. What happens with water?	Water turns milky, but crystals/grains remain	Water is a little cloudy, but crystals dissolve
4. What happens with vinegar?	Nothing	Bubbles

Have one person from each team go to the materials table and carefully carry a tray of materials back to their team. Tell students to wait until every team has its materials, and then you will go over the testing procedure together. Explain that their task is to be like Ada Twist, scientist, and ask questions and make observations to solve a science mystery! Like Ada, they will also be following safety guidelines. The first thing students should do is place a small plastic bath cup on each circle of their testing mat, which has circles labeled Mystery Mixture A and Mystery Mixture B. They should also place a craft stick next to each cup to use for stirring.

Next, review the procedure for testing the mystery mixtures by reading the directions at the top of the Mystery Mixtures data sheet together. Then have students begin testing the mixtures as they did in the Properties of Matter activity. A sample completed data sheet is shown in Table 11.3 (observations may vary).

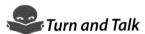 **Turn and Talk**

After students have finished testing both mystery mixtures, have them turn and talk with a partner to compare the results and observations of their tests. Be sure they refer to their Properties of Matter data sheets to come up with logical conclusions that are based on the properties of the known substances. Explain that good scientists always provide *evidence* when they make a claim. So, on their student page, they need to write more than just what they think

the two substances in the mixture are. They must provide evidence to support their conclusions. Then have students work together to fill out the conclusions and evidence statements at the bottom of the page. The best answers are as follows:

I think Mixture A contains cornstarch and sand because it turned milky, the crystals or grains didn't dissolve, and it did not bubble.

I think Mixture B contains baking soda and salt because both substances dissolved in water and it bubbled.

> **SEP: Engaging in Argument from Evidence**
> Construct an argument with evidence to support a claim.

 **Synthesizing**

Ask

? Which mystery mixture turned milky when mixed with water? (Mystery Mixture A)

? What do you think it must contain? (cornstarch)

? What is your evidence? (We observed the same thing happen with cornstarch in the Properties of Matter activity.)

? Which mixture had crystals that did not dissolve in water? (Mystery Mixture A)

? What do you think it must contain? (sand)

? What is your evidence? (We observed the same thing happen with sand in the Properties of Matter activity.)

? Which mixture had crystals that dissolved in water? (Mystery Mixture B)

? What do you think it must contain? (salt)

? What is your evidence? (We observed the same thing happen with salt in the Properties of Matter activity.)

? Which mixture bubbled when mixed with vinegar? (Mystery Mixture B)

? What do you think it must contain? (baking soda)

? What is your evidence? (We observed the same thing happen with baking soda in the Properties of Matter activity.)

? What are you still wondering? (Answers will vary.)

> **CCC: Patterns**
> Patterns in the natural world can be observed, used to escribe phenomena, and used as evidence.

Congratulate students on being great scientists and using their observations, knowledge, and skills to solve a mystery, just like Ada Twist did!

evaluate

Matter Quiz

You may want to review the three states of matter by showing the short (1:39 min.) PBS LearningMedia video called "What's the Matter?" (see the "Website" section), by having students quiz one another on vocabulary using their New Vocabulary List pages,

or by doing both. Then pass out the Matter Quiz student page. The answers are as follows:

1. Solid
2. Gas
3. Liquid
4. Liquid
5. Solid
6. C
7. D
8. E
9. B
10. A

Matter Mystery

As an additional evaluation activity, pass out the Matter Mystery student page, and have students work alone or with a partner to solve the mystery. The answers are as follows:

1. Cornstarch
2. Cornstarch does not have crystals. It turns water milky and does not bubble with vinegar.

Bonus: Students should draw a scientist on the back of their paper. Characteristics of a great scientist might include the following:

- Asks questions that lead to more questions
- Makes careful observations
- Uses tools
- Works safely
- Uses evidence to make claims
- Perseveres
- Communicates well

STEM Everywhere

Give students the STEM Everywhere student page as a way to involve their families and extend their learning. They can do the activity with an adult helper and share their results with the class. If students do not have access to these materials or the internet at home, you may choose to send the materials home or have students complete this activity at school.

Opportunities for Differentiated Instruction

This box lists questions and challenges related to the lesson that students may select to research, investigate, or innovate. Students may also use the questions as examples to help them generate their own questions. These questions can help you move your students from the teacher-directed investigation to engaging in the science and engineering practices in a more student-directed format.

Extra Support

For students who are struggling to meet the lesson objectives, provide a question and guide them in the process of collecting research or helping them design procedures or solutions.

Extensions

For students with high interest or who have already met the lesson objectives, have them choose a question (or pose their own question), conduct their own research, and design their own procedures or solutions.

After selecting one of the questions in the box or formulating their own question, students can individually or collaboratively make predictions, design investigations or surveys to test their predictions, collect evidence, devise explanations, design solutions, or examine related resources. They can communicate their findings through a science notebook, at a poster session or gallery walk, or by producing a media project.

Research

Have students brainstorm researchable questions:

? What kinds of scientists study matter?

? What kind of gas is in soda (or pop)?

? How do smells travel through the air?

Investigate

Have students brainstorm testable questions to be solved through science or math:

? Does salt dissolve faster in warm water or cold water?

? What combination of cornstarch and water makes the best oobleck?

? Survey your friends: If you could be a scientist, what kind would you be? Graph the results, then analyze your graph. What can you conclude?

Innovate

Have students brainstorm problems to be solved through engineering:

? Can you design a toy rocket that works with vinegar and baking soda?

? Can you build a model of a volcano that uses vinegar and baking soda to represent lava?

? Can you design a way to prove that air is matter (has weight and takes up space)?

Website

"What's the Matter?" (video)
*https://ca.pbslearningmedia.org/
resource/evscps.sci.phys.matter/
whats-the-matter*

More Books to Read

Beaty, A. 2013. *Rosie Revere, engineer.* New York: Abrams.
Summary: Young Rosie dreams of being an engineer. Alone in her room at night, she constructs great inventions from odds and ends. Afraid of failure, Rosie hides her creations under her bed until a fateful visit from her great-great-aunt Rose, who shows her that a first flop isn't something to fear—it's something to celebrate.

Diehn, A. 2018. *Matter: Physical science for kids.* White River Junction, VT: Nomad Press.
Summary: From the Picture Book Science series, this book provides a simple definition of *matter*, information on the states of matter, and examples of things that are not matter.

Fries-Gaither, J. 2016. *Notable notebooks: Scientists and their writings.* Arlington, VA: NSTA Press.
Summary: Take a trip through time to discover the value of a special place to jot your thoughts, whether you're a famous scientist or a student. Engaging illustrations, photos, and lively rhyme bring to life the many ways in which scientists from Galileo to Jane Goodall have used a science notebook.

Mason, A. 2005. *Move it! Motion, forces and you.* Tonawanda, NY: Kids Can Press.
Summary: This lively and easy-to-understand book explores materials—their color, shape, texture, size, mass, magnetism, and more.

Zoehfeld, K. 2015. *What is the world made of?: All about solids, liquids, and gases.* New York: HarperCollins.
Summary: Part of the Let's-Read-and-Find-Out Science series, this book uses simple text and playful illustrations to explain the differences among the states of matter and includes a "Find Out More" section with experiments designed to encourage further exploration.

Name: _____

Properties of Matter

You can be like a scientist and explore the properties of matter!

Test 1: Rub the substance between your fingers. How does it feel? Record the texture.

Test 2: Use a hand lens to look more closely at the substance. Can you see any crystals? Write yes or no.

Test 3: Use an eyedropper to add three full droppers of water to the substance. Stir with a stick for 30 sec. What happens?

Test 4: Use an eyedropper to add 10 drops of vinegar to the substance and water mixture. Stir with a stick for 30 sec. What happens?

Test	Salt	Cornstarch	Sand	Baking Soda
1. Texture (feel)				
2. Crystals? (yes/no)				
3. What happens with water?				
4. What happens with vinegar?				

Name: _____

Properties of Matter

You can be like a scientist and explore the properties of matter!

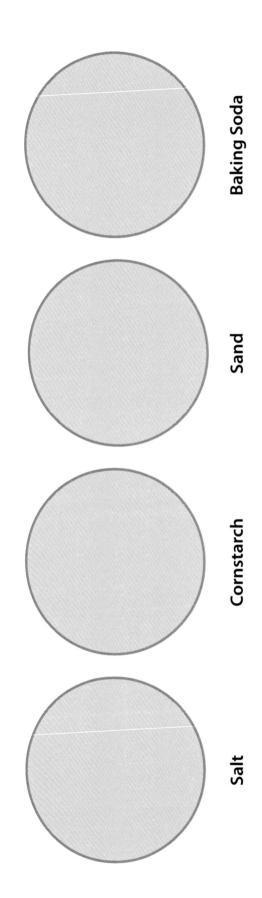

Baking Soda

Sand

Cornstarch

Salt

National Science Teaching Association

Vocabulary Cards

Gas	Solid	Dissolve	Matter	Liquid

Gas	Solid	Dissolve	Matter	Liquid

Gas	Solid	Dissolve	Matter	Liquid

Gas	Solid	Dissolve	Matter	Liquid

Gas	Solid	Dissolve	Matter	Liquid

Gas	Solid	Dissolve	Matter	Liquid

Name: _____

New Vocabulary List

Word	What It Means	Examples From the Text	Examples From the Activity
1.	Anything that has weight and takes up space		
2.	Matter that holds its size and shape		
3.	Matter that is wet and takes the shape of its container		
4.	Matter that has no shape and spreads out to fill a space		
5.	To mix a substance into a liquid until you can no longer see it		

National Science Teaching Association

Name: _____

Mystery Mixtures

You can be like a scientist and use your observations to solve a mystery!

Test 1: Rub the mystery mixture between your fingers. How does it feel? Record the texture.

Test 2: Use a hand lens to look more closely at the mystery mixture. Can you see any crystals? Write yes or no.

Test 3: Use an eyedropper to add three full droppers of water to the mystery mixture. Stir with a stick for 30 sec. What happens?

Test 4: Use an eyedropper to add 10 drops of vinegar to the mystery mixture and water. Stir with a stick for 30 sec. What happens?

Test	Mixture A	Mixture B
1. Texture (feel)		
2. Crystals? (yes/no)		
3. What happens with water?		
4. What happens with vinegar?		

I think Mixture A contains _____ and _____ because _____.

I think Mixture B contains _____ and _____ because _____.

Mystery Mixtures

You can be like a scientist and use your observations to solve a mystery!

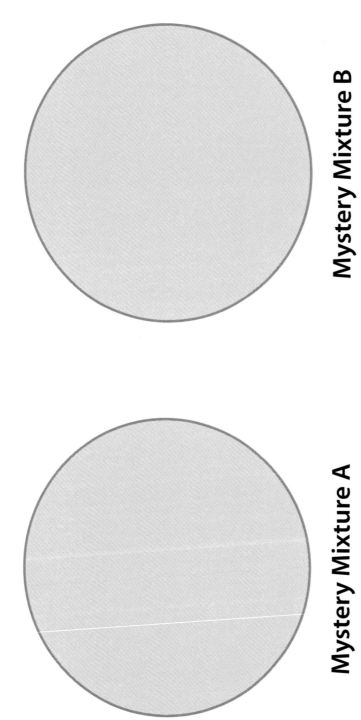

Mystery Mixture A

Mystery Mixture B

Name: _____

Matter Quiz

Write *solid*, *liquid*, or *gas* on the lines below.

Block

Air

Water

1. _____ 2. _____ 3. _____

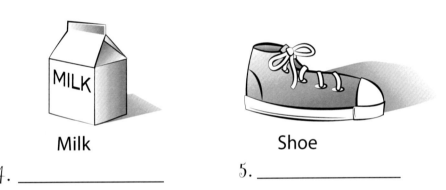

Milk

Shoe

4. _____ 5. _____

Write the letter of the definition next to each word.

6. ___ Matter   A. To mix a substance into a liquid until you can no longer see it

7. ___ Solid   B. Matter that has no shape and spreads out to fill a space

8. ___ Liquid   C. Anything that has weight and takes up space

9. ___ Gas   D. Matter that holds its shape

10. ___ Dissolve   E. Matter that is wet and takes the shape of its container

Name: _____

Matter Mystery

Ada's teacher is filling jars with salt, cornstarch, sand, and baking soda, but she forgets to put labels on the jars! She asks Ada to help her identify what's inside one of the jars. Ada looks at the mystery substance with a hand lens and does not see any crystals. She takes a small sample of the substance and mixes it with water. The water turns a milky color. Then she takes another sample, places 10 drops of vinegar in it, and observes that nothing happens. Use the chart below to help Ada solve the mystery!

Test	Salt	Cornstarch	Sand	Baking Soda
1. Texture (feel)	Rough and gritty	Slippery	Rough and gritty	Smooth
2. Crystals? (yes/no)	Yes	No	Yes	No
3. What happens with water?	Salt disappears, and water looks almost clear	Water turns milky	Sand does not disappear, and water looks cloudy	Baking soda disappears, and water looks cloudy
4. What happens with vinegar?	Nothing	Nothing	Nothing	Bubbles

1. Which substance do you think it is? _____

2. What is your evidence? _____

_____

_____

_____

Bonus: Draw a picture of a scientist on the back of this page. Then write some characteristics of a great scientist around your picture!

National Science Teaching Association

Name: _____

STEM Everywhere

Dear Families,

At school, we have been learning about properties of matter. We used our observations of different kinds of matter to solve a mystery! To find out more, ask your learner questions such as:

- What did you learn?
- What was your favorite part of the lesson?
- What are you still wondering?

At home, you can watch a short video together about how to make oobleck, which is a substance that acts like both a solid and a liquid.

 Search for "How to Make Magic Mud Oobleck" on YouTube to find the video at *www.youtube.com/watch?v=WHLCYfwa36g.*

Make your own oobleck by mixing 1 cup of water, 5 drops of food coloring, and 2 cups of cornstarch in a foil pie pan. Next, you can do a simple experiment by observing what will happen if you drop a marble from a distance of 2 feet into the pan of oobleck.

What happens when a marble is dropped into oobleck? Predict, then try it!

_____

_____

How is oobleck like a solid?

_____

_____

How is oobleck like a liquid?

_____

_____